THE FUTURE OF AN ILLUSION

Also By Rush Rankin

In Theory

Pascal's Other Wager

Bene-Dictions

The Failure of Grief

THE FUTURE OF AN ILLUSION

Rush Rankin

Etruscan Press

Etruscan Press
Wilkes University
84 West South Street
Wilkes-Barre, PA 18766
(570) 408-4546

Wilkes
University

www.etruscanpress.org

Published 2025 by Etruscan Press
Printed in the United States of America
Cover design by Logan Rock
Interior design and typesetting by Andrea Reider
The text of this book is set in Garamond Premiere.

First Edition

17 18 19 20 5 4 3 2 1

Library of Congress Cataloging-in-Publication Data

Names: Rankin, Rush, author.
Title: The future of an illusion / Rush Rankin.
Description: First edition. | Wilkes Barre, PA : Etruscan Press, 2025. | Summary: "The Future of an Illusion investigates the author's impending death as an aesthetic dilemma with ironic implications. The Future of an Illusion is a gorgeous collection, delving into the essentials of life and death in a voice that is both intimate and ethereal. The refrains woven into the poems are subtly haunting. The depth of feeling swells into striking philosophical observations. Entwining strands of narrative, lyric, and meditation, The Future of an Illusion feels completely at home in its own idiom, moving not in opposition to poetic conventions, but on another plane"-- Provided by publisher.
Identifiers: LCCN 2025020058 | ISBN 9798990767805 (paperback ; acid-free paper)
Subjects: LCGFT: Poetry.
Classification: LCC PS3568.A5715 F88 2025 | DDC 811/.6--dc23/eng/20250424
LC record available at https://lccn.loc.gov/2025020058

Please turn to the back of this book for a list of the sustaining funders of Etruscan Press.

This book is printed on recycled, acid-free paper.

In memory of my mother,
Julia Edwards Rankin

CONTENTS

ACKNOWLEDGMENTS

New American Writing

Hotel Amerika

The Flexible Persona

The Briar Cliff Review

I find that stooping over the microscope
affects my heart.

—Charles Darwin

I

The person who is likely soon to be dead
walks out into his front lawn at night
to savor the soothing quiet of all his neighbors
breathing as they sleep in order to confirm
what it means to be alive.

In the dazzling light
of the afternoon sun, fluttering about
in the tree limbs hanging over the street,
birds in a forest fire are trying to escape
their beating wings.

I mean, everybody I know, everybody I don't know,
is dying, some in a village trying
to escape bombs dropped from the sky, others quietly,
as though rehearsing the invisible,
my last breath still
the secret only I perform. A vaguely dying poet remains,
of course, too weak and hopeless to displace his death
by its depiction, unless attuned to the Japanese dilettante,
that ritual haiku, as though just breathing on a mirror.
Even to what we don't know we're related in a way
we don't know, like a drunk
tiptoeing in the dark.
When the rude force of things overwhelms thinking
what's specific becomes more important
than the systemic shifting of thought.

Knowing so little of everything that's knowable, I only celebrate,
          like Rousseau, the precious delights of my narrow focus,
as though exclamations justify themselves. The stunned victim
of some obscure devastation,
                                        exposed by a sudden flash of light,
speaks only to protect his silence, though that intense focus might
have a delicate implication. The past, more expansive than perception,
limits our conclusions to mere glimpses. Our searching awareness
shifts in the dark from one distraction to the next. Evolution itself
enacts the discreet maneuver of discrete people who stumble
across the future. For the sleeping person
                                                            who wakes up dead,
The ultimate non sequitur, the lucky, painless oblivion of dying,
while asleep, cancels its expectation, that weakness, that death,
                                    that Kafka also thought was embarrassing.

Every important truth must endure its own ambiguity,
  the way a living person, who eventually dies,
faces the eerie feeling of being alive.
                All thinking
    suffers the fact of its own flesh, that baby pissing
       in his diaper, screaming for the mother,
who's already dead. That Aristotle says it's only safe
to judge the success of your life right before dying
sounds like a joke that's really funny
                if you're not
    actually dying. Compare a sudden sneeze
to a volcano that destroys a whole village of Italians
    whose charred remains are now a museum.

Note: a poem more than dogma, more than fashion,
more than the glib version of film noir,
that dried blood
at the abattoir, that dull truth, that couture princess
sipping vermouth, discovers its overwhelming sadness:
that souvenir sword my father left on the floor
right outside his wife's bedroom door.
I mean, the aniconic poem
I can't write must deflect
the sadness, must ignore the neglect, of my troubled brother,
who died alone without my knowing.

Though lurching from anodyne to accusation,
a succinct diction a sign of affection, though detecting
a toxic potential,
like a forensic dog
at the airport, I absorb the lively pretension
of the artistic life, as though showing
a horse's taste for dressage, to test,
to dramatize, with that propriety and protocol,
with its odd moral focus,
some secret conclusion,
that involves a CT scan, that reads the carbonized scroll
of a remote, ghostly culture, erased by its future.

The ineffable poet's narrow personality neglected generous inclinations
in order to protect his life from impositions
that might have deepened his poetry,
but required too much attention
to other people, he confesses.
As in a moral fable, his sight now is blurred by the flickering aura
of schematic shapes on the surface of his eye, like broken glass
falling from a high window
into clear water. In evolution an eye
emerges from an amoeba, like Darwin from his study. That spider
skating across the surface of water, tracing a path
that disappears, demonstrates, by disappearing, what seeing means.
Among all the tedious disruptions, all those violations,
I can't really speak
of what's most amazing, that endearing, glowing person, her smile.

A life, to avoid disappearing when asserted,
involves a compelling fact, as in the act of giving birth,
that baby twitching about, as every smiling person
reaches out. Since a life gets lived
no matter what it means,
no matter what happens, the fact of life is more fundamental
than a thought. That means everybody thinking is quietly
in mourning all the time, which means each serious truth
faces its own ambiguity, which means each person,
who eventually dies,
faces the ironic feeling
of being alive. Of course, that thudding sound of dirt
dropped on a coffin attracts the attention of birds
in the surrounding trees.

That my lively family doesn't suffer the self-conscious
agony typical of poetry implies that obituaries
for them are not the kind of abstract sadness
that poets avoid. The genre itself
could be improved
by describing the odd way a person explodes
inside himself so violently the whole world itself
disappears in that tribute to everything
that's delicate. Sometimes
I hold my breath in front
of a mirror, as though my image, sliding off the surface,
as I pass, exposes a ghost.

II

In the initial excursion, the flurry of events
muting all conclusions, attuned to the resonance,
the reverberation, of flesh,
that flushed face,
those beached whales, a feral poetry indulges
its avidity, a peculiar acidity, the felt world itself
so precise it rhymes, those electrical charges fusing
one phoneme to another,
that wet brain flashing
in the darkness, like an ancient eel at the bottom
of the ocean.

Of course, a poem more than dogma,
more than fashion,
more than the glib version
of film noir, that dried blood at the abattoir, that dull truth,
that couture princess sipping vermouth, discovers
its overwhelming sadness:
that souvenir sword
my father left on the floor right outside
his wife's bedroom door, my mother holding her breath.

Now an ancient person with ruined knees who creeps
down the stairs as carefully as a thief I'm almost nothing
but the past, that future moment
when a friend deletes
my number from his phone. (In the attic there's a photo
of one self-conscious immigrant staring blankly
at the future.) The more constraining norms
of a formal proof, like
the more demanding norms
of an expansive proof, I avoid, as one tribute to my limitations.
I mean, immersed in time, like a fish in water,
what I see through I can't see.

Though you can't measure everything to confirm a specific
(say, after a hurricane, when you're drinking),
                                                            it doesn't matter,
because the test itself implies the options, just as one finger
on your hand suggests the others, each glove a declaration.
Every conscious person, of course, dies facing the impossible
solitude and horror and blankness
                                                  of his vanishing, which means
        that everybody thinking is quietly in mourning all the time.

The vast clutter of trash in the oceans seen from the sky,
all those plastic bags, those inert dolphins,
often means nothing to people
who ignore the effect
of picnics seen from a blanket. A horse stands alone
in the street in an ancient country as invisible jets
pass overhead. In the vast swollen expanse of sky
it's the invisibility of jets the visible reverses, the visible
exposes, by exploding. What remains is the empty nothing
of absolute light shining in the absolute emptiness
of its shining: a dead horse,
dead family, didactic,
among the rubble. A furious wind flips the pages of a book
among the rubble.

My lamp, granting access to the speed of light, its halo glowing,
I turn off and on, without thinking, off and on without thinking,
the ultimate fact of the universe invoked,
then cancelled,
without thinking. A narrow focus on point of view
distorts our unstable immersion in the thickness of events.
As Napoleon strolled across the field at dusk,
the nervous sentries he passed
ignored bodies
still falling through the earth. Of course, every thought
involves the impression of a body in sand, which a wave erases,
each idea that surface distinction that disappears.

A modern monk thinking of reincarnation while sitting in a robe
on the temple porch at night, as burning cadavers float down
        the river, sees that having only one life is like riding
a stationary bike across the country. That one day
                                                            the Buddha left
his famous umbrella behind, hanging by itself in air, as a model
         for poems, stands in contrast, in the German army, in WWI,
to Martin Heidegger, who deployed weather balloons to help steer
poison gas toward the French. Addicted only to grand sensations,
like Wagner, whose anti-Semitism disgusted Nietzsche, Heidegger
           never cried, though the smoke of crematoria drifted across
his country. Picture Heidegger visiting
                                                  an extermination camp
          after World War II among all the tourists, each death
          the word he never spoke, as the smoke from crematoria
                                                drifted across his country.

The silent politics of a Chinese drawing
of black crows on the whiteness of the sky
control the point of view by directing attention
away from the peasants who are bending over
to plant rice at the horizon.
Facing a future
as abstract as silhouettes in a fire, the artist thinks
the shadowy figures he traces on paper
are what's real. His sketch exposes what before
was only implied
or hidden in the mind of a person who died.
That thudding sound of dirt
dropped on a coffin
attracts the attention of birds in the surrounding trees.

As a storm expands across an electronic map
the weather impresario points like an explorer
            at the spot where a plane
                                                  has crashed.
That's one version of the terrible pressure
          of events. The spiraling double helix
          of thinking includes pluralistic options
within the binary aspects of a unitary system
          that has the consistent structure of water,
          affection, and despair,
                                          whose ambiguity,
          more than any idea, defines the real options
          of logic, despite the terrible pressure of events.

Each heady, sophistic ideal faces the erasure
of itself, its convictions, minus the conclusions
        of a terrible battle,
                minus the concussions
of a terrible battle, in some glorified confusion,
that struggle to survive the pressure of events.
        Death, not just an outcome, nor the future,
but implicit in every breath, that invisible gun
            in the distance,
                    affects every truth.
            Should you crash your car into a buffalo
            standing in the road you'll merely confirm
                    the pressure of events.

Since a life gets lived no matter what it means, no matter
what happens, the fact of life is more fundamental
than a thought. That each tense person,
who eventually dies,
faces, day after day, the haunted feeling of being alive,
is what the official obituary survives, since each person,
who eventually dies, faces every day that haunted feeling
of being alive. That implies that everybody thinking is quietly
in mourning all the time. The nervous poet
in front of a mirror
fears his image, sliding off the surface, as he passes, exposes
that ghost to himself. The precise obituary is a kind of scream.

III

Smiling in a hotel room one stranger insists
to another that the phone beside the bed
            that keeps ringing
                                    is not a problem.
That doesn't mean intellectuals undressing
in a lighted room don't assume incorrectly
that the meaning of bodies is exhausted
by the function of mirrors. A cell phone
still ringing beside the bed might sound
            desperate, when it really isn't,
though a physical fact
                                is the context
            for all thought, as when a woman
off in the distance is staring at her phone.

The failed writer prefers the mundane editor so freed
            from the ethereal sky of decent people who pray
            he publishes failed poetry written at a posh resort
in Jamaica that idealizes poets
                                        who can afford to travel.
The intention of making an automobile whose purpose
is to transport people from one place to another succeeds
when the manufacturing process
                                        builds a car in which
you might flee the apocalypse. If, when you step on the gas,
the car disappears, you've reached the middle of a poem.

A life, to avoid disappearing when asserted, involves a compelling fact,
as in the act of giving birth, that baby twitching about, as everybody
in the room reaches out.

Since a life gets lived no matter
what it means, no matter what happens, the fact of life is more important
than a thought. Every agonizing truth must endure some ambiguity,
the way a living person, who eventually dies, faces the eerie feeling
of being alive. That the sky is large enough to absorb everybody
in the world breathing out at the same time shows what's obvious
provides a cosmic scale

for a monstrous event
that nullifies our ability to think. Only a fable can present the indirect
meaning of the gnostic version of what's only implied, not unlike
the situation of a skier buried underneath an avalanche of snow,
who sees a faint blue light before he dies.

That a poet puts books in a furnace to test readers who pick words
from ashes merely obscures the fact of the Holocaust,
which does require, in contrast, that the performance artist
burn people who've been gassed.
Schematic sculpture
is the vacuous alternative at Dachau that one tourist on vacation
has compared to the vagueness of the act of breathing. As usual,
the Holocaust remains a blur, a photograph of naked bodies
thrown into a pile, unless the crazed artist actually does burn people
who've been gassed. Few people these days are serious enough
about art to scream at everybody they meet
for the rest of their lives.
In contrast, the poet that extends his prosthesis to greet a friend,
a friend unnerved by intangible gestures, a soldier still feeling
his phantom leg, honors the drama of some invisible struggle.

Each change we see exists as part of a larger context
in which no change changes the ultimate limit
of all possible change. Each person enacts one version
of the incipient options
that precede any action.
Unlike mystics, I dive into only one part of the ocean
at a time. The completeness of a great poem I only read
incompletely. Sharing that kind of aesthetic restraint
with people who study poetry
more profoundly
than the science of dark holes increases
the chance of my being told about a hotel
that poets like, every building a state of mind.

In evolution, an eye emerges from an amoeba, like Darwin
from his study. A spider skating across the surface of water,
tracing a path that disappears,
demonstrates, by disappearing,
what seeing means. The staccato tapping of rain
in the cemetery is the only applause an old man
has the right to expect when thinking about people
in coffins. Each dying person dissolves, of course,
from the inside out, without detecting the moment
his body has become only its weight.
Saying this indulges
that self-obsession that's monitored by the actual logic
of mirrors that fail to reflect the air itself.

IV

Floating in the ocean, my eyes open,
my sight dazed by the intense sky,
          I glanced toward the beach,
          where my aunt and cousins,
under an umbrella,
                    were drinking
gin, and laughing, while playing
a word game. Years later, after
the funeral, I emptied my portion
of her remains
               from a plastic bag.
That ghostly dust, like the residue
of a remote explosion, drifted
               across the lawn.

At the airport returning home
after the funeral, I joined the larger funeral
of other travelers standing
in the boarding area
to watch quietly on TV as the huge hurricane
in New Orleans floated dead bodies
down the flooded streets.
In my initial class back home, I stared
at the students, who were waiting for me
to speak. That the flurry of chalk dust
suggested the blackboard
hadn't been cleaned
for years explains why the first words I wrote
disappeared in the ghostly haze
of all those erasures, like breath against the sky.

Stretched out, a drink within reach in a gently rocking train,
                    the world a scenic diversion out the window,
                    a vacationing poet, attuned to implications,
          traveled through Europe.
                                        On the leather seats folded out
          into a bed, the passengers, sharing grapes and jokes,
reclined together, then slept, as the train rumbled through
                    the darkness, like a refrain. Earlier that day,
                              the poet glimpsed
                                                  through his window
                              the accident of a sports car and a tractor
            on a country road, a child in a daze standing nearby,
                                                  as the train flew past.

Later, in a terrorist alert, in a suspicious beret
and dark glasses, when disembarking a ferry
    from Ireland, the poet
            was stopped
    by a surly official who resented vetting
    yet another academic, who, it turned out,
only wrote poems, just as one secretive child,
living near the tracks, thought
            each person
    a secret movie, and each passing train
       the haunting sound of another life.

In a quirky, off-centered aesthetic, as archaic as an apothecary,
a great British actor said, when asked for tips on acting:
"Whenever you can, sit down," a diversion ideal
for the ineffable,
off-handed Buddha,
who practiced dying all his life. My frowning mother
teaching English, her words spiraled out from moving chalk,
her authority a papal bull, the elect
freed from the dull.
Overwhelmed by the dense compendium
of ideas, I wrote, during break, with Mother's help, my paper
on E. M. Forster's soulful hero, who carried a wasp outside.

Dazed boys at the neighborhood park, slouched on the seats
of a swing, can't see, in their evening sleepiness, what they watch
without seeing, all those vague, implicit options, that suspense,
those hazy scenes on a television
                                        in the house across the street.
In a furious naval battle, those remote explosions, as one ship
          in the storm slowly sinks, all those arms extended,
          those silent screams floating still above the wreckage,
another ship sails its cannons into port, as a kind of lecture
          in an empty, echoing hall.
                                        As the attendant standing
in the aisle mimes a plane's emergency protocol right before
take-off, one passenger, to avoid thinking about the vastness
                                   of the sky, is already reading a novel.

In each clichéd mea culpa I celebrate myself
at a party other people can join, as if humor
is a form of sadness, or sadness,
even more sadly,
a form of humor or regret really a form of hope.
I regret my limits, of course, especially
in the self-indulgent lament of this secret elegy,
my serious, dignified mother
having died
in her sleep. I mean, it's not just the pathos
of distance, that empty, echoing space, implicit
in telephone calls, that I seldom overcome.

In the funeral home as we passed a mirror
free of our reflections, my mother collapsed,
my once lively, feverish, devoted sister,
now dead. Dead.
Outside the nearby grocery,
I couldn't avoid breathing the cigarette smoke
of clerks exhaling on their break.
One tattooed girl's tangled, orange hair
drooped over the cavity where an eye normally
would be. When a country singer at home,
at his window, whispers
an elegy to himself,
mumbles a song to himself, after the terrible call,
his daughter now dead, the sadness of his words
passes through glass like a view.

V

One kind of poem includes the fireflies in a bottle,
the fireflies and the bottle, the staccato flashing
of fireflies in a bottle, set adrift in a pond,
like a moral problem in a storm,
as hysterical children
run in and out of the shadows at night.
In New Guinea, fashioned from twigs and cloth,
with tiny shells for eyes, small pig sculptures,
placed near a child's bed, ensure the fulfillment
of nightly dreams. A belief born of objects and gestures
helps resolve what's ambiguous in an appeal to spirits.
That a friend gave me
two dream pigs for my office
to endow my writing with the tenderness of a trance
seems not to have worked.

Having a wonderful child in his life so compelling
the poet didn't even think about poetry except when writing
a poem that took that affection for granted.
The clarity
of his own world oddly involves
the eventual death of everybody he knows
while working still to face what nobody
can explain. That means everybody thinking
is quietly in mourning all the time.
The serious toddler arranging word magnets
on the refrigerator door underneath
the endearing photos
of the other children produces a coherent non sequitur
as intriguing as cartoon mermaids on an ancient map.

The double helix itself, floating within other fleshy membranes,
vaguely organizing the general functions of thinking, activates
one option rather than another. As we streak

                                        through a sentence,

        that sequence, a paratrooper falling through air, one word
        at a time, our logic is both freed and restricted by the life
we're living. Not seeing a tree for the forest, not seeing the forest
        for a tree, we need to get closer or step away. If the forest
explodes, we asked the wrong question. Since a life gets lived
no matter what it means, no matter what happens,

                                                the fact of life

is more fundamental than a thought. We absorb without noticing
                        the arbitrary values that shape our solipsism
without noticing, the way a storm defines the person who's drowning.

Referring to something means I'm thinking, which means
I'm alive, which means I'll keep thinking about everything
but death, which is unthinkable, until I don't know
I'm dead. That the word "death"
defies all norms
of reference makes it useless for people
who aren't dead. That skier buried
underneath an avalanche of snow was dazed
by a faint blue light before he died. That I'm already older
than everybody who's dying is like knowing a secret
I shouldn't, which I can't understand or survive
or share with anybody else.
In the process of dying
I've become alert to endearing people in sentimental movies
that I prefer to problems that can't be solved
before the movie ends.

At the funeral, a torrent of rain crashing down,
everybody started sprinting for their cars, as one
huge drop exploded against the preacher's shoe.
My bitter father, now abruptly
                                        buried, my mother,
running with everybody else, hurriedly took a seat
          in a polished car driven by her oldest friend
          to a resort on the coast. There she absorbed
          the calming effect of those redundant waves
pounding against the shore.
                                    At Christmas we relaxed,
          even telling jokes, now that the painful fear
of the past was just the ghost of our future, as all
          those waves kept slamming against the shore.

An aesthetic theory indulging paradox induces a thinker
to celebrate the epiphany of an ancient priest who claims
that God's existence is only proven
when logic transcends
its limitations. In this tricky calculation,
the idea of the infinite power of God collapses
if God is subjected to the dull norms of human thought,
as in the Woody Allen joke: "I'd never join a club that would
have somebody like me as a member." A God or poem
not in fact more profound than what anybody thinks
is just another delusion that's obscured by thinking.
If God is something I can think,
I'm that God, which sadly
is the case. Troubled by ideal explanations, those
ideal negations, I trust the self-indulgent mumbling
I recommend to everybody else looking up at the sky.

Every real judgment involves so much delusion,
ignorance, and bias, each version soon dissolves
within itself, like a book of poetry
left out in the rain.
My brother-in-law's lungs filling up with fluid,
as he's drowning inside himself, his devoted sister
at the hospital diverts his attention by absorbing,
within herself, the bitter terror of his disbelief,
so that helping him puts her own life in danger. Still.
His dying was a different problem
than what he thought.
I mean, after the fact some things aren't as important
as they seemed, though that too involves more dying,
rather than merely a book of poetry left out in the rain.

My wonderful aunt's liberal concern for people in pain
was constrained by a culture generally free of lynchings,
but little else. The golden whiskey in a blue Mexican glass
on her bedside table set the options.
Only the sadness
induced by drinking, despair granted its special status,
offered her relief. Her bearish husband, polite, arrogant,
and patronizing, a diplomat, was clever enough
to justify golf, while obscuring the force and source
of all real problems. Even today the oppressive,
dangerous buffoonery of one flamboyant man,
his preening, pouting version
of Mussolini, seems
something from the past, all those people laughing
at a cocktail party for a psychopath,
as a delicate poet watches TV late at night.

Of course, every serious truth must endure
some ambiguity the way a living person,
who eventually dies, faces the haunted feeling
of being alive. That means
everybody thinking
is quietly in mourning all the time. Someday soon
there will be a cough that never stops or a swelling
or a bleeding that never stops or a pain
that never stops as I disappear in a scream
that nobody can hear. A few days ago, a doctor said:
melanoma. That I feel
the sadness of myself
more than the misery of everybody else
is not surprising to people who know me.

VI

Between each subject and verb, I disappear
without disturbing the implications of grammar
when my mother dies in her sleep,
her wasted corpse
a silhouette of bones. Two people determined to live
together, until one dies, sounds strange, even morbid,
a way of relating the exact terms of an empty hope
to the fact of despair. That eventual horror is what
all couples share. In the casual method
of groping about, a guy, who relies on his hands
to gauge the effect of darkness, for years,
gets used to touching what's no longer there.
That's the final result of that
glib flirtation one night
in a bar. Often such a person doesn't notice what can't
be touched, nor what makes touching a kind of prayer.

There is the flickering of light on green leaves fluttering
under the streetlamp when surrounded by shadows
in the moody nostalgia of the evening. People arising
each morning note the darkness
has disappeared,
that expanding light still an explosion still heard
at the beginning of time. Each dazed person sitting
on the side of his bed, just before standing up, is stunned
by the delicacy of light. In that same mood, old blackboards,
covered in the chalk residue of hazy notations,
have been arranged into an art installation in the gallery
at my college. To retrieve from that kind of ghostly surface
my own past ideas requires a subtle attention
to the ineffable,
as when a football, spiraling through space each Sunday,
connects one kind of hope to another.

The momentary absolute of affection doesn't change until later
in a different, equally objective context, which is comparable
to the earlier circumstance, not because it's different, which it is,
but because it's only itself, no matter the distractions. Of course,
          everything attuned to the bias of ethics
                                                            must survive
          the unconscious paradigms of social shifts that define
the unconscious focus of bias, as every important truth suffers
some ambiguity, the way a living person, who eventually dies,
          must face, day after day, the strange feeling
                                                              of being alive.
               (That thudding sound of dirt dropped on a coffin
          attracts the attention of birds in the surrounding trees.)
That the frail houses on the side of our hill were like a refrain
               in country music meant that each regret was more
than just another beer, even as we leaned our elbows on the bar.

I do hope to savor that sweet nostalgia that preserves
what's important, as when my dearest aunt stepped off
            the porch that last time into the slanted shadows
of trees at dusk, those dull frogs,
                                    around her small pond,
            repeating their awkward lament, like tiny Buddhas
squatting in the dark, those delicate moths, that crumble
when touched, hovering in the faint light from the kitchen.
My aunt's Siamese cat coiled about itself seemed dazed
by the pleasure of a secret rumination that was typical
of the Egyptians, who shaved their eyebrows to mourn
the death of a cat. The stylization of sadness
                                              is a weakness
            of poets too, said my smiling aunt. In their grandeur
                        and gravitas poets still think the weather
a function of that point where the sky touches the earth.

Whether we die alone or not, all deaths, after the fact,
are the same, even at Dachau. I mean, in the emptiness
of death, we're all equally empty, though that's not
any kind of ideal.
What's invisible
is what everybody is breathing. That thudding sound
of dirt dropped on a coffin
attracts the attention of birds
in the surrounding trees. My own feelings now
so delicate, I mute the TV during anxious scenes
in a film and would avoid poetry this bleak
were it not my own. Everybody thinking
is quietly
in mourning all the time. That a state employee
fails to answer the phone only when it rings
suggests the ultimate limit of all politics.

My lamp, granting access to the speed of light, its halo glowing,
I turn off and on, without thinking, off and on without thinking,
the ultimate fact of the universe invoked,
then cancelled,
without thinking. A narrow focus on point of view
distorts our unstable immersion in the thickness of events.
As Napoleon strolled across the field at dusk,
the nervous sentries he passed
ignored bodies
still falling through the earth. Of course, every thought
involves the impression of a body in sand, which a wave erases,
each idea that surface distinction that disappears.

In the giddy solipsism of self-assertion, the driver of a speedboat
roars past floating docks that rise and fall
in tune to the curling waves he leaves behind. Everybody holds on
to the sides of their canoe as he flashes by.
A largesse of options
sometimes overwhelms a delicate calculation the way a storm
defines the person who's drowning. A poet trying
to pick up a piece of paper on the floor that's actually
a sliver of light is pleased by the unexpected irony
of perception, as though one kind of angel is only implicit, only
animated, when immersed in the mundane. In the scope
of his life he's that person in a parachute
in a war zone
who discovers, when diving at night
out of a plane, that he's not coming down at that place on the map
he had studied.

When talking disdainfully to my mother to justify
my sleazy, bohemian life, I said, "Well, Faulkner
was a bum," to which she responded,
as in a koan,
"Yes, but not every bum was Faulkner."
In her genteel voice, a Buddhist monk raking
the sand of an ideal garden to celebrate
a pure focus, I finally see, in the severe
ethics of precision itself, the accidental source
of what's honest, what's generous,
her death
that thought I can't survive. That now I'm dead
is something I'm afraid to say.

ABOUT THE AUTHOR

In addition to one book on aesthetics, *In Theory*, the poet has published three books of poetry: *Pascal's Other Wager* (2006), *Bene-Diction* (winner of The Vassar Miller Prize, 2003), and *The Failure of Grief* and has appeared in a number of literary magazines: *New American Writing, Antioch Review, Paris Review, The Yale Review, Triquarterly, Pleiades, Mudfish, Gargoyle, Confrontation,* and *Hotel Amerika*. The poet's academic degrees are from Duke University, The University of North Carolina, and The Writer's Workshop, University of Iowa. He has taught English at Virginia Tech, the U. of Iowa, the U. of Missouri at Columbia, the Kansas City Art Institute, and the U. of Missouri at Kansas City.

Books from Etruscan Press

Zarathustra Must Die | Dorian Alexander
The Disappearance of Seth | Kazim Ali
The Last Orgasm | Nin Andrews
Son of a Bird | Nin Andrews
Drift Ice | Jennifer Atkinson
Crow Man | Tom Bailey
Coronology | Claire Bateman
Viscera | Felice Belle
Reading the Signs and other itinerant essays | Stephen Benz
Topographies | Stephen Benz
What We Ask of Flesh | Remica L. Bingham
The Greatest Jewish-American Lover in Hungarian History | Michael Blumenthal
No Hurry | Michael Blumenthal
Choir of the Wells | Bruce Bond
Cinder | Bruce Bond
The Other Sky | Bruce Bond and Aron Wiesenfeld
Peal | Bruce Bond
Scar | Bruce Bond
Until We Talk | Darrell Bourque and Bill Gingles
Big Time | Rus Bradburd
Poems and Their Making: A Conversation | Moderated by Philip Brady
Crave: Sojourn of a Hungry Soul | Laurie Jean Cannady
Toucans in the Arctic | Scott Coffel
Sixteen | Auguste Corteau
Don't Mind Me | Brian Coughlan

Wattle & daub | Brian Coughlan
Body of a Dancer | Renée E. D'Aoust
Generations: Lullaby with Incendiary Device, The Nazi Patrol, and How It Is That We | Dante Di Stefano, William Heyen, and H. L. Hix
Ill Angels | Dante Di Stefano
Aard-vark to Axolotl: Pictures From my Grandfather's Dictionary | Karen Donovan
Trio: Planet Parable, Run: A Verse-History of Victoria Woodhull, and Endless Body | Karen Donovan, Diane Raptosh, and Daneen Wardrop
Scything Grace | Sean Thomas Dougherty
Areas of Fog | Will Dowd
Romer | Robert Eastwood
Wait for God to Notice| Sari Fordham
Bon Courage: Essays on Inheritance, Citizenship, and a Creative Life | Ru Freeman
Surrendering Oz | Bonnie Friedman
Funeral Playlist | Sarah Gorham
Nahoonkara | Peter Grandbois
Triptych: The Three-Legged World, In Time, and Orpheus & Echo | Peter Grandbois, James McCorkle, and Robert Miltner
The Candle: Poems of Our 20th Century Holocausts | William Heyen
The Confessions of Doc Williams & Other Poems | William Heyen
The Football Corporations | William Heyen
A Poetics of Hiroshima | William Heyen
September 11, 2001: American Writers Respond | Edited by William Heyen
Shoah Train | William Heyen
American Anger: An Evidentiary | H. L. Hix

As Easy As Lying | H. L. Hix
As Much As, If Not More Than | H. L. Hix
Chromatic | H. L. Hix
Demonstrategy: Poetry, For and Against | H. L. Hix
First Fire, Then Birds | H. L. Hix
God Bless | H. L. Hix
I'm Here to Learn to Dream in Your Language | H. L. Hix
Incident Light | H. L. Hix
Legible Heavens | H. L. Hix
Lines of Inquiry | H. L. Hix
Rain Inscription | H. L. Hix
Shadows of Houses | H. L. Hix
Wild and Whirling Words: A Poetic Conversation | Moderated by H. L. Hix
All the Difference | Patricia Horvath
Art Into Life | Frederick R. Karl
Free Concert: New and Selected Poems | Milton Kessler
Who's Afraid of Helen of Troy: An Essay on Love | David Lazar
Black Metamorphoses | Shanta Lee
Sign & Breath: Voice & the Literary Tradition | Edited by Shanta Lee and Philip Brady
Mailer's Last Days: New and Selected Remembrances of a Life in Literature | J. Michael Lennon
Parallel Lives | Michael Lind
The Burning House | Paul Lisicky
Museum of Stones | Lynn Lurie
Quick Kills | Lynn Lurie
Synergos | Roberto Manzano

The Gambler's Nephew | Jack Matthews
American Mother | Colum McCann with Diane Foley
The Subtle Bodies | James McCorkle
An Archaeology of Yearning | Bruce Mills
Arcadia Road: A Trilogy | Thorpe Moeckel
Venison | Thorpe Moeckel
So Late, So Soon | Carol Moldaw
The Widening | Carol Moldaw
Clay and Star: Selected Poems of Liliana Ursu | Translated by Mihaela Moscaliuc
Cannot Stay: Essays on Travel | Kevin Oderman
White Vespa | Kevin Oderman
Also Dark | Angelique Palmer
Fates: The Medea Notebooks, Starfish Wash-Up, and overflow of an unknown self | Ann Pedone, Katherine Soniat, and D. M. Spitzer
The Dog Looks Happy Upside Down | Meg Pokrass
Mr. Either/Or | Aaron Poochigian
Mr. Either/Or: All the Rage | Aaron Poochigian
The Shyster's Daughter | Paula Priamos
Help Wanted: Female | Sara Pritchard
American Amnesiac | Diane Raptosh
Dear Z: The Zygote Epistles | Diane Raptosh
Human Directional | Diane Raptosh
I Eric America | Diane Raptosh
50 Miles | Sheryl St. Germain
Saint Joe's Passion | J.D. Schraffenberger
Lies Will Take You Somewhere | Sheila Schwartz
Fast Animal | Tim Seibles

One Turn Around the Sun | Tim Seibles
Voodoo Libretto: New and Selected Poems | Tim Seibles
Rough Ground | Alix Anne Shaw
A Heaven Wrought of Iron: Poems From the Odyssey | D. M. Spitzer
American Fugue | Alexis Stamatis
Variations in the Key of K | Alex Stein
The Casanova Chronicles | Myrna Stone
Luz Bones | Myrna Stone
In the Cemetery of the Orange Trees | Jeff Talarigo
The White Horse: A Colombian Journey | Diane Thiel
The Arsonist's Song Has Nothing to Do With Fire | Allison Titus
Bestiality of the Involved | Spring Ulmer
The Waw | Jacqueline Gay Walley
Silk Road | Daneen Wardrop
Sinnerman | Michael Waters
The Fugitive Self | John Wheatcroft
YOU. | Joseph P. Wood
Leaves Borrowed from Human Flesh | Abigail Ardelle Zammit

Etruscan Press Is Proud of Support Received From

Wilkes University

Ohio Arts Council

The Stephen & Jeryl Oristaglio Foundation

Community of Literary Magazines and Presses

National Endowment for the Arts

Drs. Barbara Brothers & Gratia Murphy Endowment

Founded in 2001 with a generous grant from the Oristaglio Foundation, Etruscan Press is a nonprofit cooperative of poets and writers working to produce and promote books that nurture the dialogue among genres, achieve a distinctive voice, and reshape the literary and cultural histories of which we are a part.

Etruscan Press
www.etruscanpress.org
Etruscan Press books may be ordered from
Consortium Book Sales and Distribution
800.283.3572
www.cbsd.com

Etruscan Press is a 501(c)(3) nonprofit organization.
Contributions to Etruscan Press are tax deductible
as allowed under applicable law.
For more information, a prospectus,
or to order one of our titles,
contact us at books@etruscanpress.org.

www.ingramcontent.com/pod-product-compliance
Lightning Source LLC
Jackson TN
JSHW030726291125
94561JS00001B/7
9798990767805